A Star is Born

design by Dick Martin

Leisure Arts Inc. • Maumelle, Arkansas

MUSICAL STAR

NL	COLOR
07	pink - 2 yds
20	yellow - 20 yds
26	green - 8 yds
*	black Fr. Knot - 1 yd

*Use 2-ply yarn.

MUSICAL STAR
Size: 5½"w x 5½"h x 1"d
Supplies: Worsted weight yarn or Needloft® Plastic Canvas Yarn (refer to color key), one 10½" x 13½" sheet of clear 7 mesh plastic canvas, #16 tapestry needle, one music button, one ½" pink pom-pom, one ¼" pink pom-pom, and 12" length of ⅜"w green ribbon
Stitches Used: Backstitch, French Knot, Gobelin Stitch, Overcast Stitch, Scotch Stitch, and Tent Stitch
Instructions:
1. Photo model was stitched using worsted weight yarn. Follow chart and use required stitches to work Front. Work stitches indicated by double lines on chart by inserting needle in same holes twice for complete coverage. Work Back with yellow Tent Stitches.
2. Tack pom-poms to Front using pink yarn.
3. With wrong sides together, use yellow yarn to join side and bottom edges of Front to Back. Insert music button between Front and Back. Use yarn color to match closest stitching area to join remaining edges of Front to Back.
4. Refer to photo for placement and thread ribbon through Front and Back. Knot and trim ribbon ends.

Front/Back
(36 x 37 threads)
(Cut 2, Stitch 1)

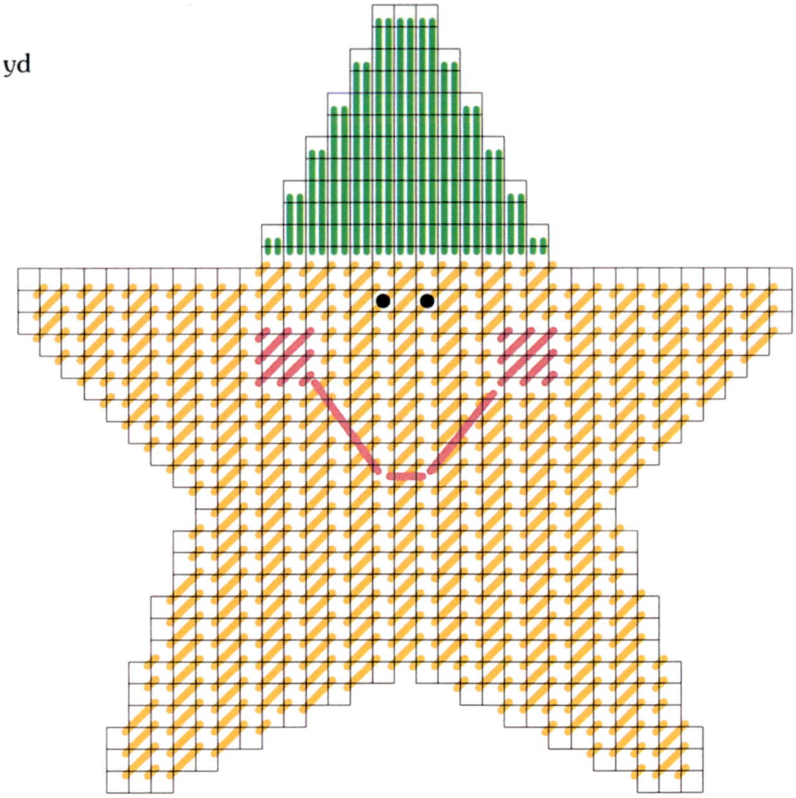

SMALL BOX

NL	COLOR
20	yellow - 4 yds
26	green - 11 yds
36	blue - 14 yds
41	white - 10 yds
41	white Fr. Knot

SMALL BOX
Size: 5"w x 3¼"h x 3¾"d
Supplies: Worsted weight yarn or Needloft® Plastic Canvas Yarn (refer to color key), one 10½" x 13½" sheet of clear 7 mesh plastic canvas, and #16 tapestry needle
Stitches Used: French Knot, Gobelin Stitch, Mosaic Stitch, Overcast Stitch, and Tent Stitch
Instructions:
1. Photo model was stitched using worsted weight yarn. Follow charts and use required stitches to work Small Box pieces.
2. For Bottom, cut a piece of plastic canvas 24 x 32 threads. (**Note:** *Bottom is not worked.*) Join Long Sides to Short Sides along short edges using white yarn. Join Bottom to Sides.

Short Side (24 x 21 threads) (Stitch 2)

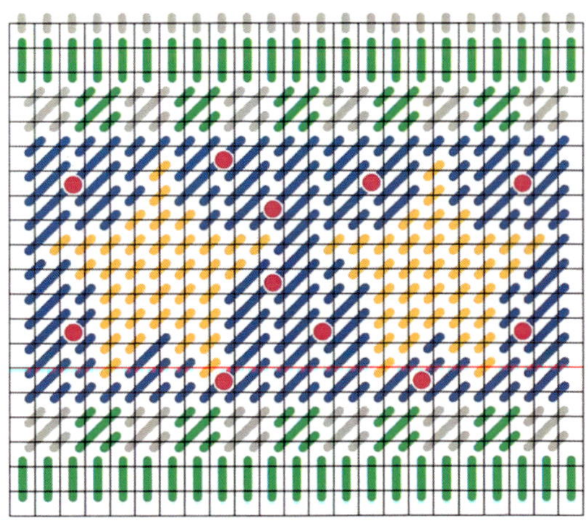

Long Side (32 x 21 threads) (Stitch 2)

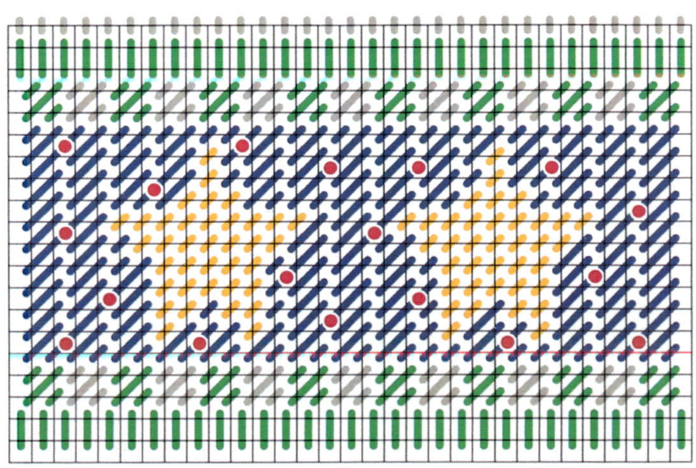

DOOR SIGN

NL	COLOR
00	black - 1 yd
07	pink - 1 yd
20	yellow - 11 yds
26	green - 3 yds
36	blue - 6 yds
41	white - 16 yds
41	white Fr. Knot

DOOR SIGN
Size: 7"w x 7¾"h
Supplies: Worsted weight yarn or Needloft® Plastic Canvas Yarn (refer to color key), one 10½" x 13½" sheet of clear 7 mesh plastic canvas, #16 tapestry needle, one ¾" pink pompom, and 16" length of ¾"w blue satin ribbon
Stitches Used: Backstitch, French Knot, Gobelin Stitch, Overcast Stitch, Scotch Stitch, and Tent Stitch
Instructions:
1. Photo model was stitched using worsted weight yarn. Follow chart and use required stitches to work Door Sign.
2. Refer to photo for placement and thread ribbon ends through Door Sign. Tie a knot in each ribbon end. Tack pom-pom to Door Sign using pink yarn.

Door Sign (46 x 52 threads)

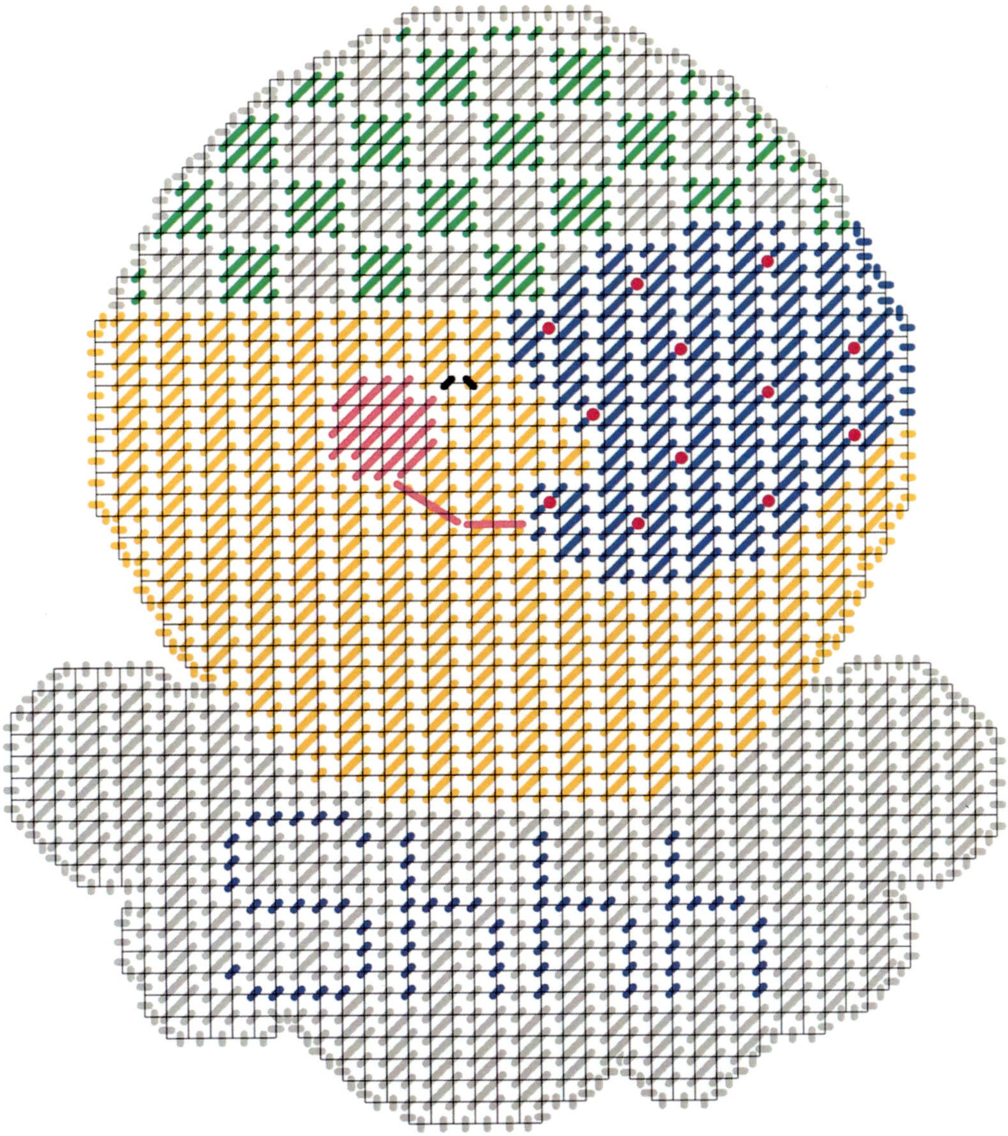

MOBILE

NL	COLOR	NL	COLOR
00	black - 2 yds	41	white - 32 yds
07	pink - 2 yds	56	flesh - 3 yds
17	gold - 3 yds	*	black Fr. Knot
20	yellow - 21 yds	17	gold Fringe
26	green - 10 yds	41	white Fr. Knot
36	blue - 4 yds		

*Use 2-ply yarn.

MOBILE

Size: 11"w x 26¼"h

Supplies: Worsted weight yarn or Needloft® Plastic Canvas Yarn (refer to color key), two 10½" x 13½" sheets of clear 7 mesh plastic canvas, #16 tapestry needle, 1" dia bone ring, pink pom-poms (¼", ½", and 1"), and nylon line

Stitches Used: Backstitch, Diagonal Mosaic Stitch, French Knot, Fringe Stitch, Gobelin Stitch, Overcast Stitch, Scotch Stitch, and Tent Stitch

Instructions:

1. Photo model was stitched using worsted weight yarn. Follow charts and use required stitches to work Mobile pieces. For hair on Baby On Swing, separate each strand of Fringe into plies. Refer to photo and use needle to separate plies until the desired look is achieved.
2. With wrong sides together, use gold yarn to join Baby Hair to Baby On Swing.
3. Refer to Diagram for placement and use white yarn to tack side and bottom edges of Cloud A to Moon. Insert Baby between Cloud A and Moon. Use green yarn to tack Baby to Moon.
4. Cut two 8" lengths of green yarn. Knot one end of each yarn length. Refer to photo to thread yarn lengths through Baby On Swing and Large Star at ❤'s. Run loose ends of yarn under backs of stitches on wrong side of Large Star to secure.
5. Refer to Mobile Diagram and use nylon line to assemble Mobile pieces.
6. Refer to photo for placement and tack pom-poms to Moon and Large Star using pink yarn.

Cloud A (28 x 14 threads)

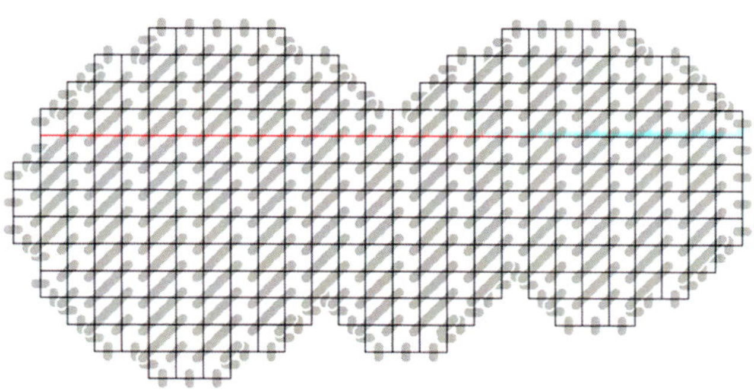

Cloud B (28 x 14 threads)

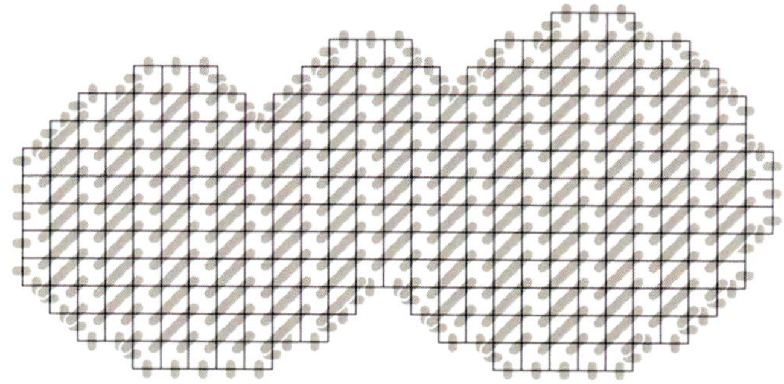

Cloud C (28 x 14 threads)

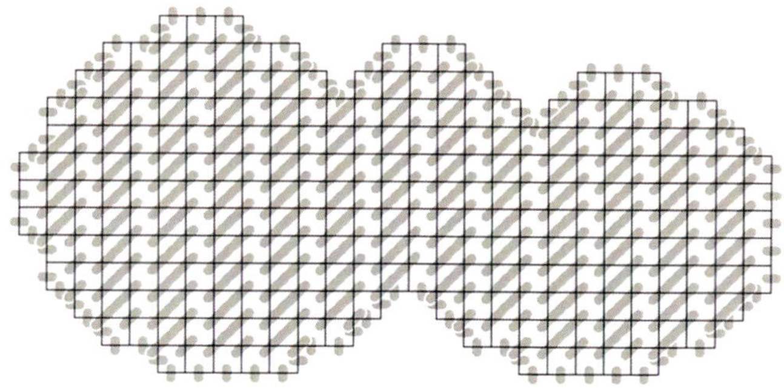

Diagram

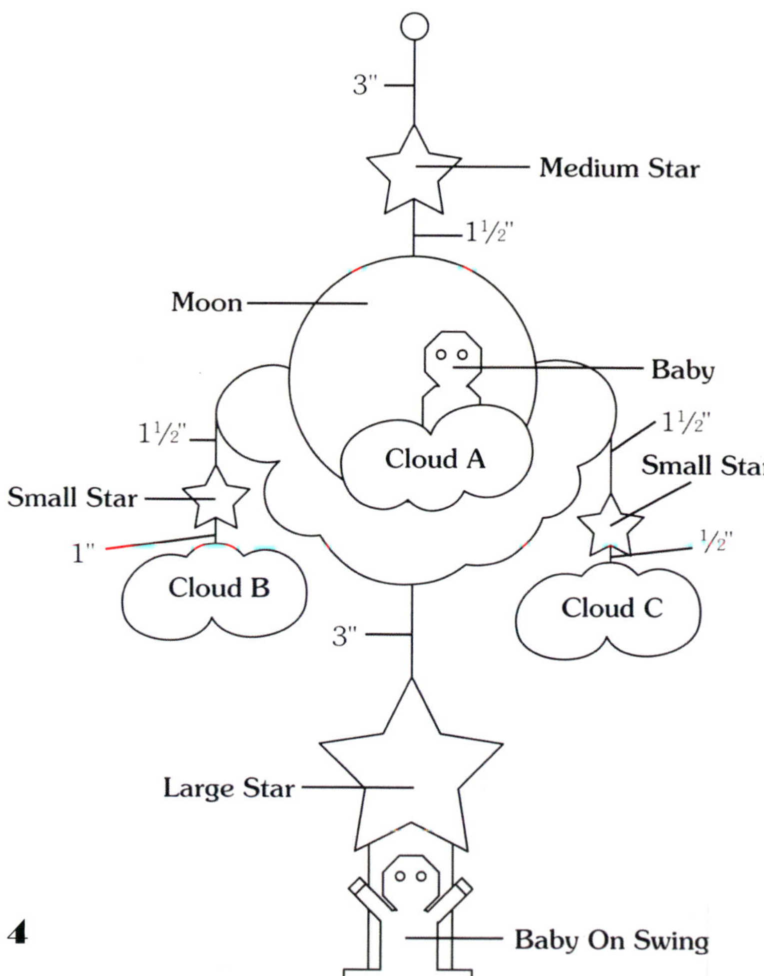

MOBILE

NL	COLOR
00	black - 2 yds
07	pink - 2 yds
17	gold - 3 yds
20	yellow - 21 yds
26	green - 10 yds
36	blue - 4 yds

NL	COLOR
41	white - 32 yds
56	flesh - 3 yds
*	black Fr. Knot
17	gold Fringe
41	white Fr. Knot

*Use 2-ply yarn.

MOBILE
Size: 11"w x 26¼"h
Supplies: Worsted weight yarn or Needloft® Plastic Canvas Yarn (refer to color key), two 10½" x 13½" sheets of clear 7 mesh plastic canvas, #16 tapestry needle, 1" dia bone ring, pink pom-poms (¼", ½", and 1"), and nylon line
Stitches Used: Backstitch, Diagonal Mosaic Stitch, French Knot, Fringe Stitch, Gobelin Stitch, Overcast Stitch, Scotch Stitch, and Tent Stitch
Instructions:
1. Photo model was stitched using worsted weight yarn. Follow charts and use required stitches to work Mobile pieces. For hair on Baby On Swing, separate each strand of Fringe into plies. Refer to photo and use needle to separate plies until the desired look is achieved.
2. With wrong sides together, use gold yarn to join Baby Hair to Baby On Swing.
3. Refer to Diagram for placement and use white yarn to tack side and bottom edges of Cloud A to Moon. Insert Baby between Cloud A and Moon. Use green yarn to tack Baby to Moon.
4. Cut two 8" lengths of green yarn. Knot one end of each yarn length. Refer to photo to thread yarn lengths through Baby On Swing and Large Star at ❤'s. Run loose ends of yarn under backs of stitches on wrong side of Large Star to secure.
5. Refer to Mobile Diagram and use nylon line to assemble Mobile pieces.
6. Refer to photo for placement and tack pom-poms to Moon and Large Star using pink yarn.

Cloud A (28 x 14 threads)

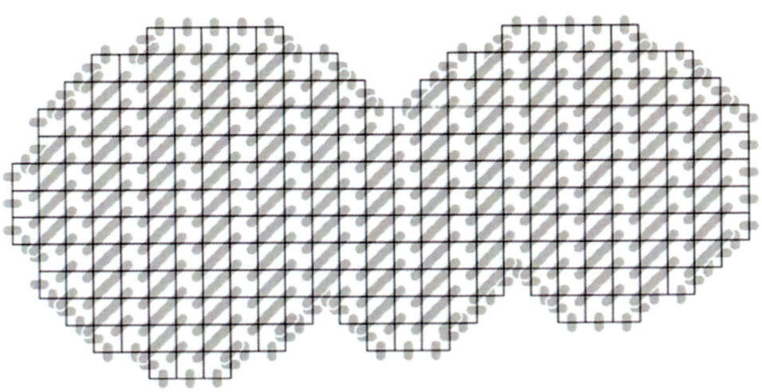

Cloud B (28 x 14 threads)

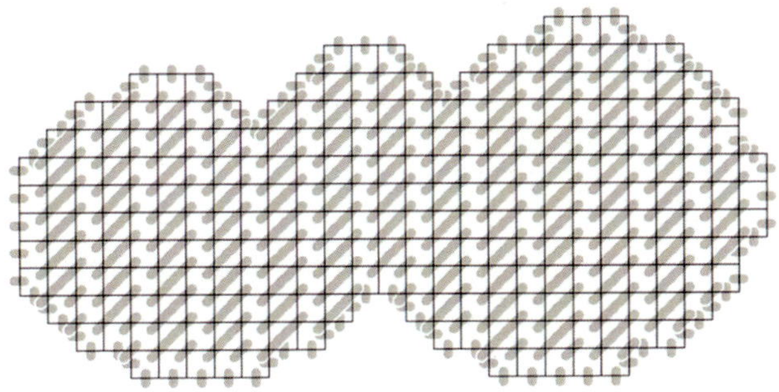

Cloud C (28 x 14 threads)

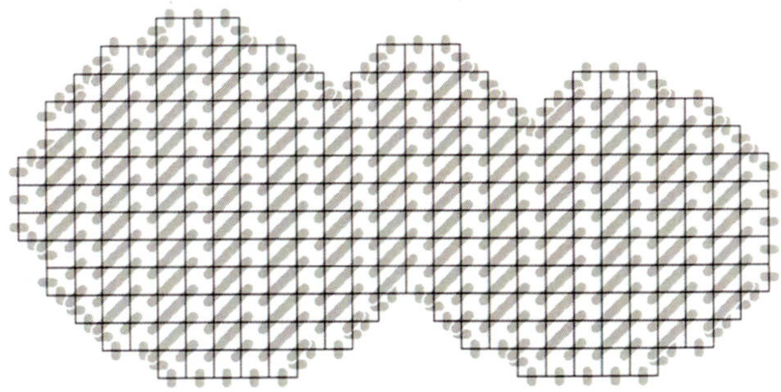

Diagram

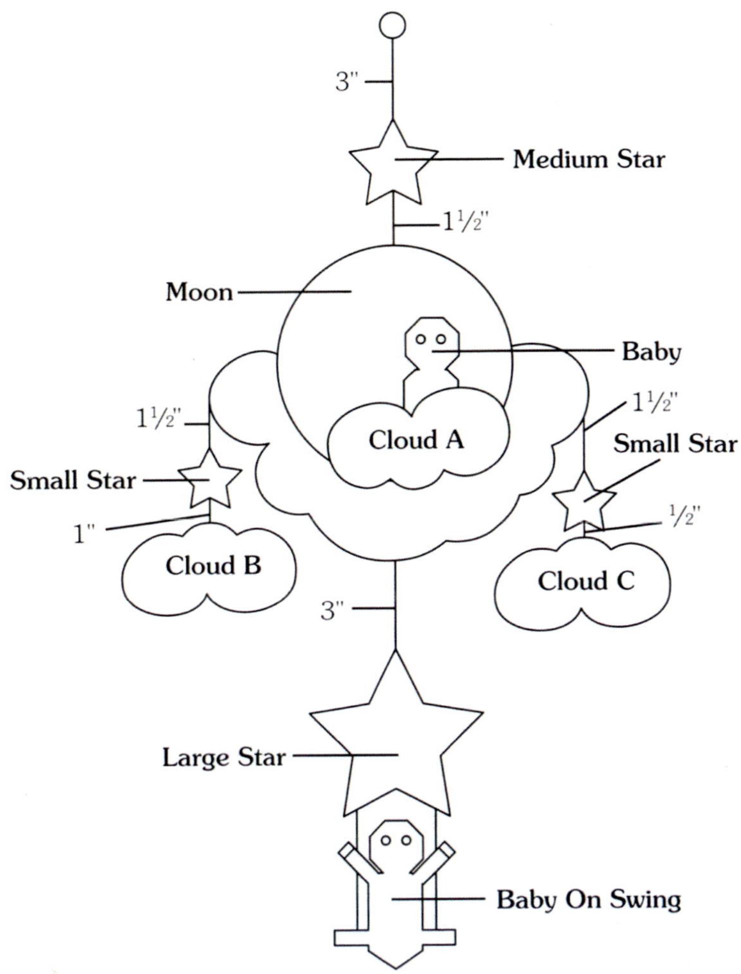

FRINGE STITCH

Fold an 8" length of yarn in half. Thread needle with loose ends of yarn. Take needle down at 1, leaving a 1" loop on top of the canvas. Come up at 2, bring needle through loop, and pull tightly ***(Fig. 5)***. Trim strands ½" from knot. A dot of glue on back of fringe will help keep stitches in place.

Fig. 5

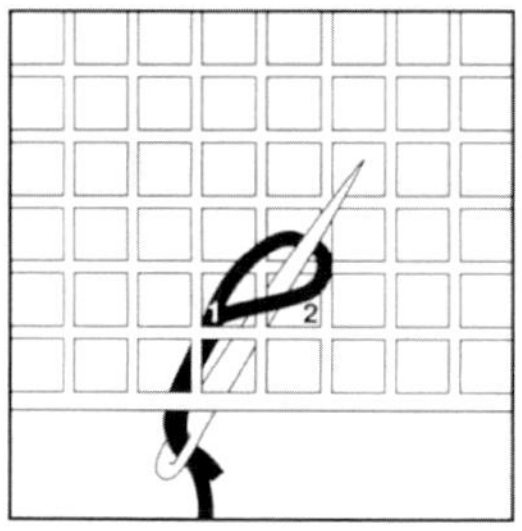

GOBELIN STITCH

This basic straight stitch is worked over two or more threads or intersections. The number of threads or intersections may vary according to the chart ***(Fig. 6)***.

Fig. 6

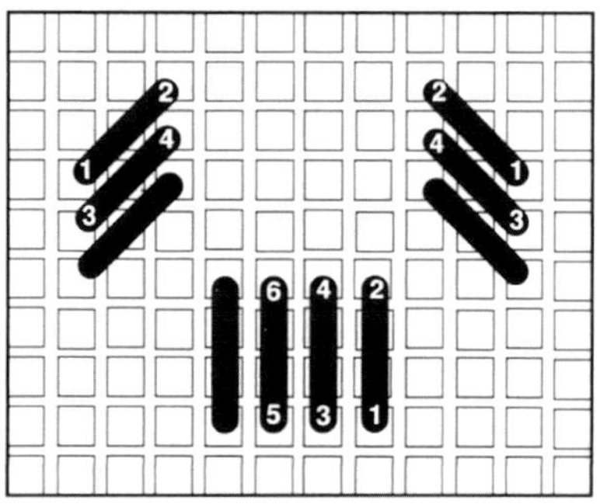

MOSAIC STITCH

This three stitch pattern forms small squares ***(Fig. 7)***.

Fig. 7

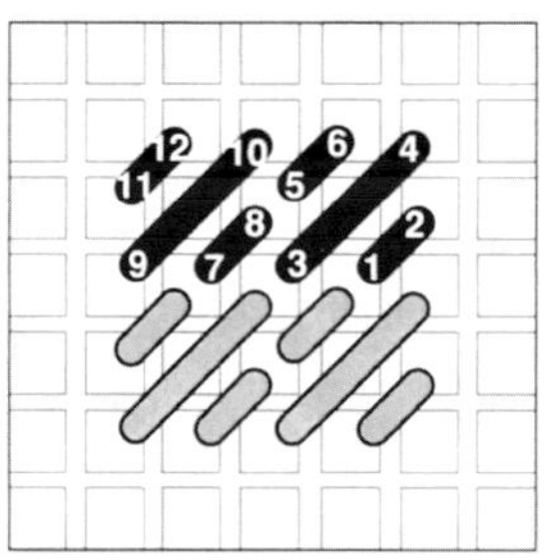

OVERCAST STITCH

This stitch covers the edge of the canvas and joins pieces of canvas ***(Fig. 8)***. It may be necessary to go through the same hole more than once to get an even coverage on the edge, especially at the corners.

Fig. 8

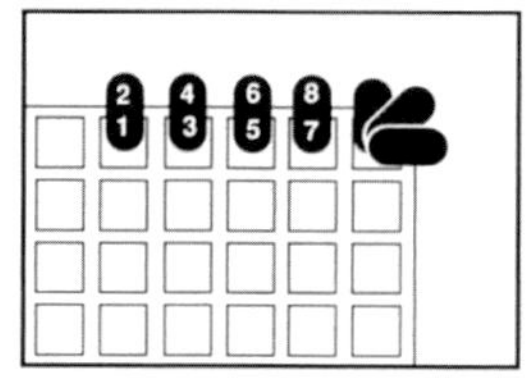

SCOTCH STITCH

This stitch may be worked over three or more threads and forms a square. **Fig. 9** shows it worked over four threads.

Fig. 9

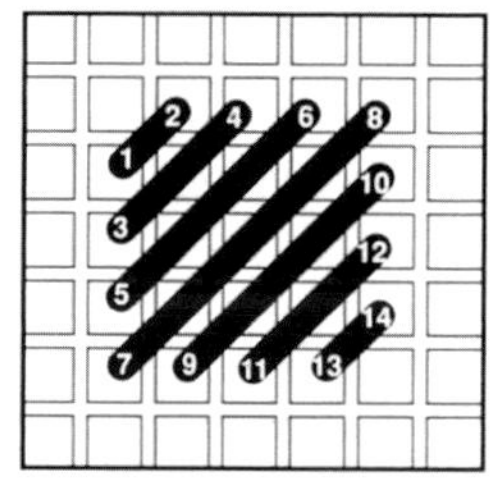

TENT STITCH

This stitch is worked over one intersection as shown in **Fig. 10**. Refer to **Fig. 11** to work the **Reversed Tent Stitch**.

Fig. 10

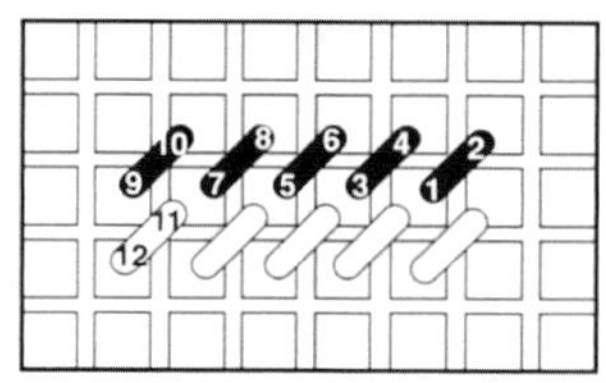

Fig. 11

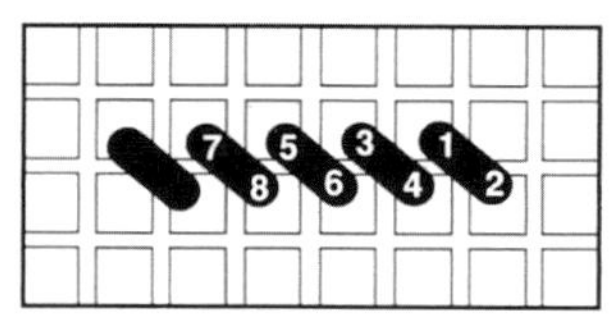

A STAR IS BORN

GENERAL INSTRUCTIONS

1. Fig. 1, page 18, shows how to count threads accurately. Follow charts to cut out pieces.

2. Backstitches used for detail ***(Fig. 2,*** *page* 18***)*** and French Knots ***(Fig. 4,*** *page* 18***)*** are worked over completed stitches.

3. Overcast Stitches ***(Fig. 8)*** are used to cover edges of pieces and to join pieces.

We have made every effort to ensure that these instructions are accurate an complete. We cannot, however, be responsible for human error, typographica mistakes, or variations in individual work.

Instructions tested and cover items made by Virginia Cates and Janice Gordon.

Medium Star (16 x 17 threads)

Large Star (30 x 29 threads)

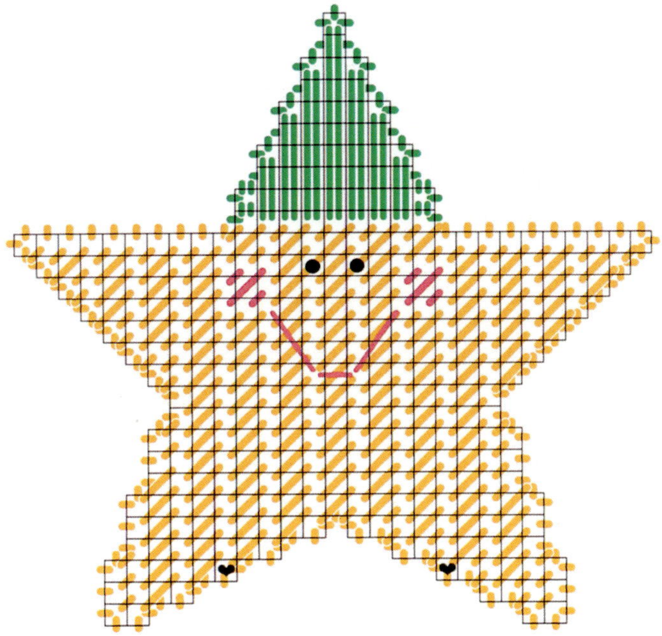

Small Star
(12 x 13 threads) (Stitch 2)

Baby (17 x 17 threads)

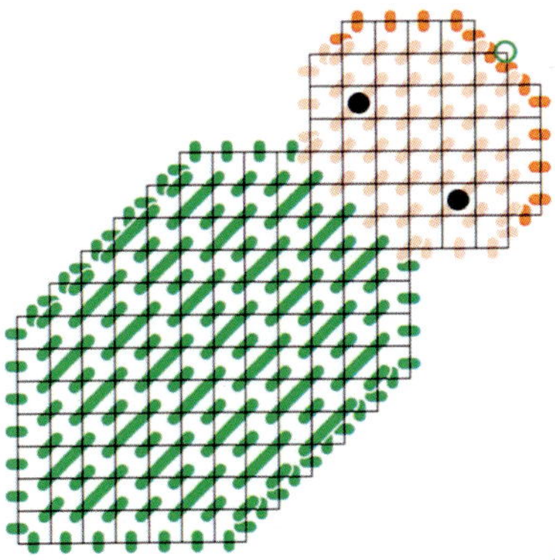

Baby On Swing
(17 x 17 threads)

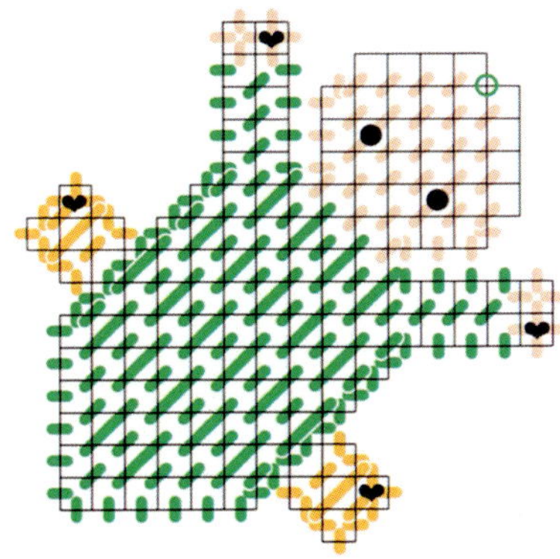

Moon (46 x 52 threads)

Baby Hair
(7 x 7 threads)

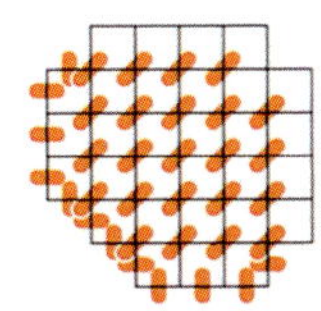

TISSUE BOX COVER

NL COLOR

- 07 pink - 2 yds
- 17 gold - 1 yd
- 20 yellow - 17 yds
- 26 green - 2 yds
- 36 blue - 46 yds
- 41 white - 25 yds
- 56 flesh - 2 yds
- * black Fr. Knot - 1 yd
- 41 white Fr. Knot
- 17 gold Fringe

*Use 2-ply yarn.

TISSUE BOX COVER
Size: 4¾"w x 5¾"h x 5¼"d
(Note: Fits a 4½"w x 5¼"h x 4½"d boutique tissue box.)
Supplies: Worsted weight yarn or Needloft® Plastic Canvas Yarn (refer to color key), two 10½" x 13½" sheets of clear 7 mesh plastic canvas, #16 tapestry needle, one ½" pink pom-pom, and one ¼" pink pom-pom
Stitches Used: Backstitch, Diagonal Mosaic Stitch, French Knot, Gobelin Stitch, Overcast Stitch, and Tent Stitch
Instructions:
1. Photo model was stitched using worsted weight yarn. Follow charts and use required stitches to work Tissue Box Cover pieces. For hair on Baby, separate each strand of Fringe into plies. Refer to photo and use needle to separate plies until the desired look is achieved.
2. Refer to photo for placement and tack pom-poms to Front using pink yarn.
3. Use blue yarn for all joining. Join Sides along long edges. Join Front to Sides. Join Top to Front and Sides.
4. Match ▲'s and use white yarn to tack side and bottom edges of Cloud to Front. Insert Baby between Cloud and Front.

Baby (17 x 17 threads)

Top (32 x 32 threads)

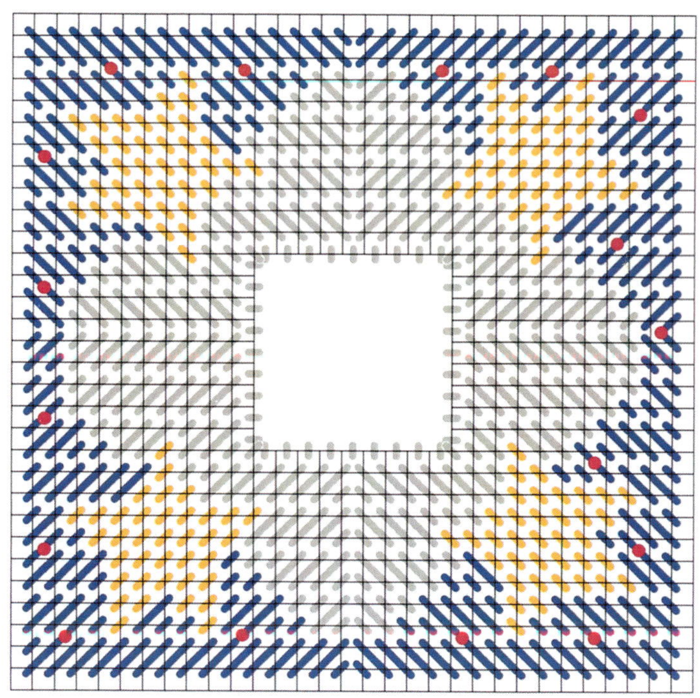

Cloud (32 x 13 threads)

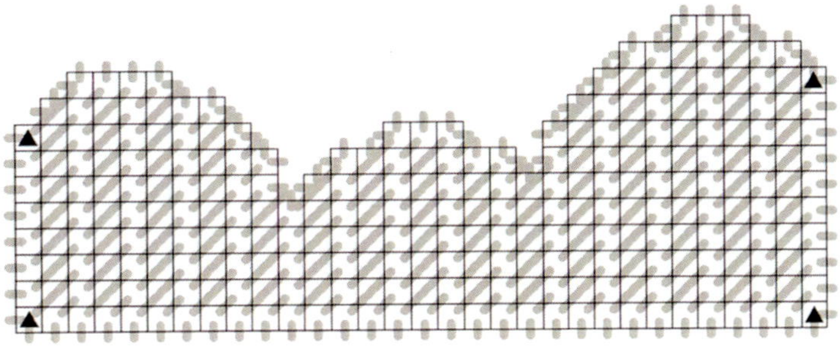

Front (32 x 38 threads)

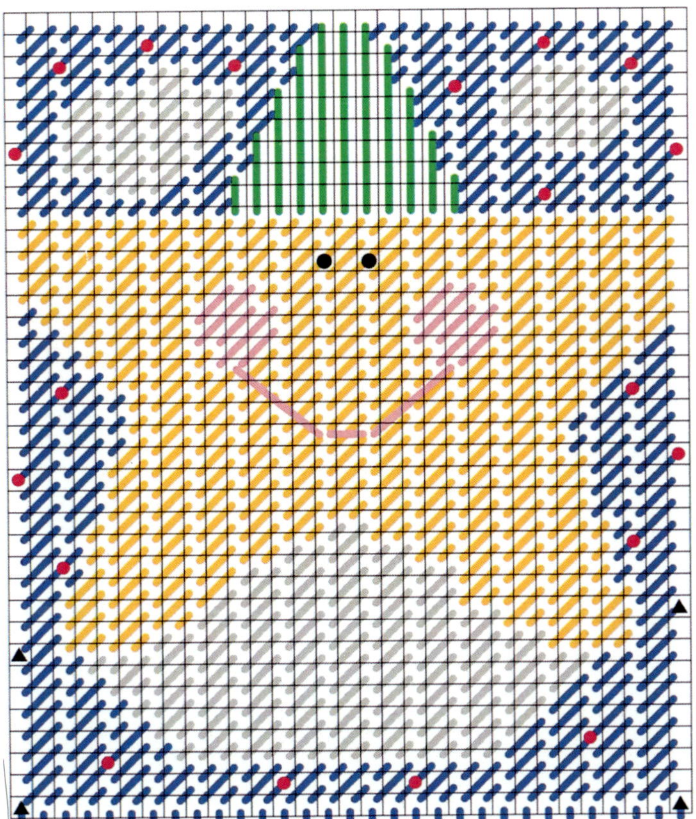

Side (32 x 38 threads) (Stitch 3)

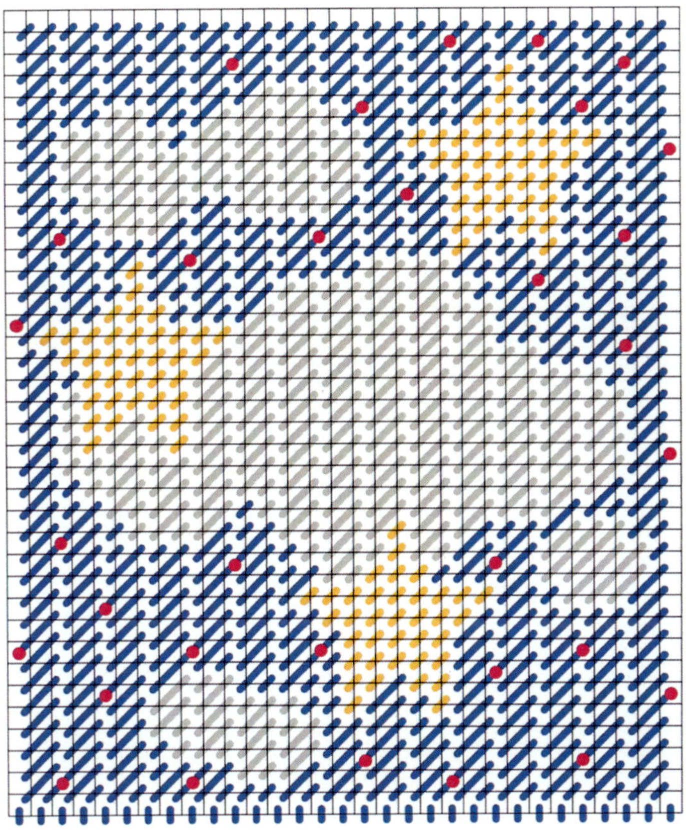

LARGE BOX

NL	COLOR	NL	COLOR
07	pink - 3 yds	41	white - 27 yds
20	yellow - 37 yds	*	black Fr. Knot - 2 yds
26	green - 5 yds	41	white Fr. Knot
36	blue - 68 yds		

*Use 2-ply yarn

LARGE BOX
Size: 13¾"w x 4"h x 7¼"d
Supplies: Worsted weight yarn or Needloft® Plastic Canvas Yarn (refer to color key), five 10½" x 13½" sheets of white 7 mesh plastic canvas, #16 tapestry needle, eight ½" pink pom-poms, and eight ¼" pink pom-poms
Stitches Used: Backstitch, French Knot, Gobelin Stitch, Mosaic Stitch, Overcast Stitch, and Tent Stitch
Instructions:
1. Photo model was stitched using worsted weight yarn. For Bottom, cut a piece of plastic canvas 90 x 46 threads. For Insert Bottom, cut a piece of plastic canvas 89 x 45 threads. (***Note:*** *Bottom and Insert Bottom are not worked.*) Follow charts and use required stitches to work Large Box pieces.
2. Join Long Sides to Short Sides along short edges using blue yarn. Join Long Sides and Short Sides to Bottom using blue yarn. Refer to photo for placement and tack pom-poms to Long Sides and Short Sides using pink yarn.
3. Use white for all remaining joining. Join Insert Long Sides to two Insert Short Sides along short edges.
4. For Center, join the two remaining Insert Short Sides along one long edge.
5. Refer to Diagram A and match ★'s to join one Divider to each side of Support through three thicknesses. Repeat for remaining two Dividers.
6. Refer to Diagram B and match ♥'s to join Support to one Insert Short Side. Match ♥'s to join Support to Center through three thicknesses. Join Center and Dividers to Insert Long Sides.
7. Refer to Diagram C to place Insert inside Large Box. Join Insert to Large Box along top edges.

Diagram A

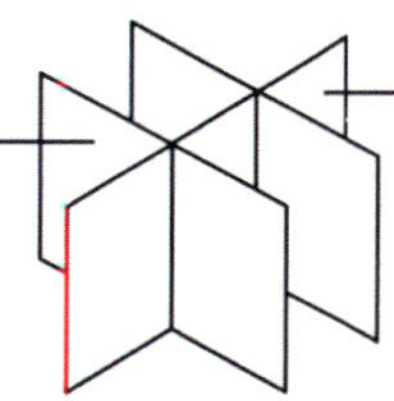

Diagram B

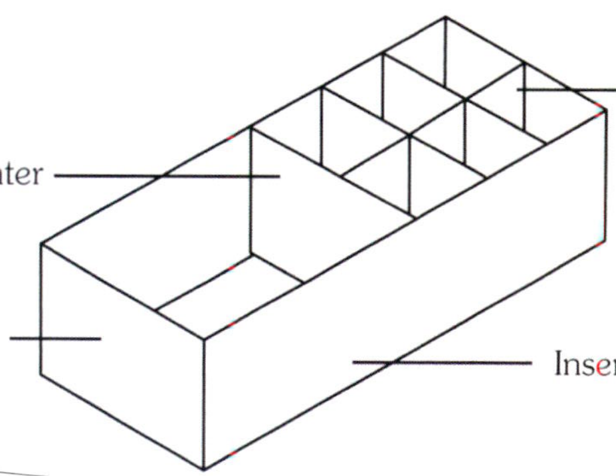

Diagram C

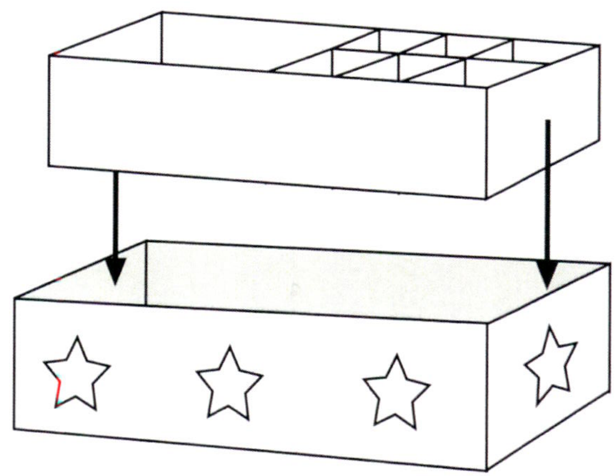

Long Side (90 x 26 threads) (Stitch 2)

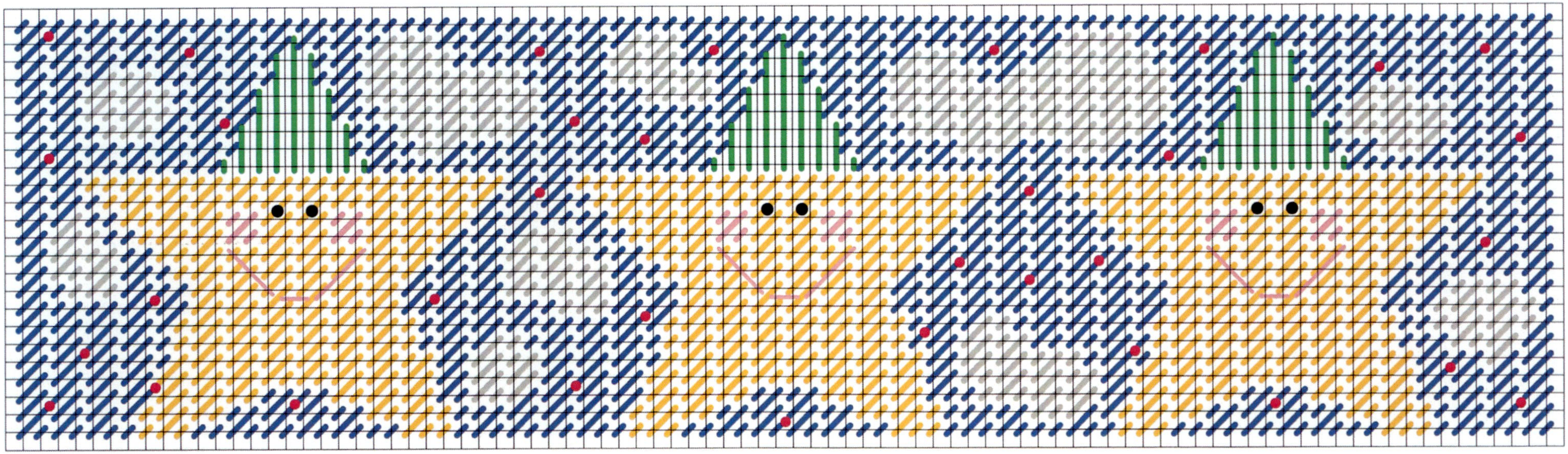

Short Side (46 x 26 threads) (Stitch 2)

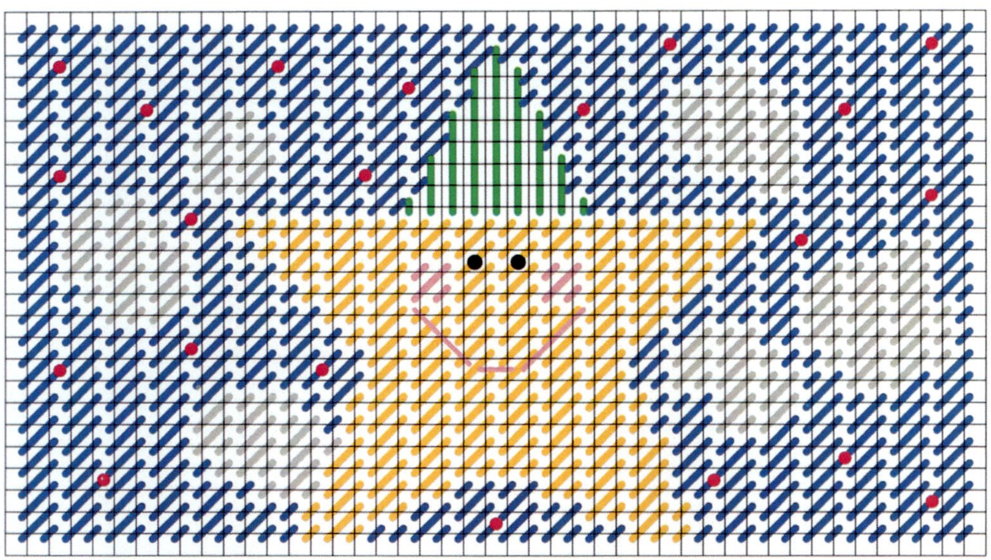

Divider (22 x 25 threads) (Cut 4)

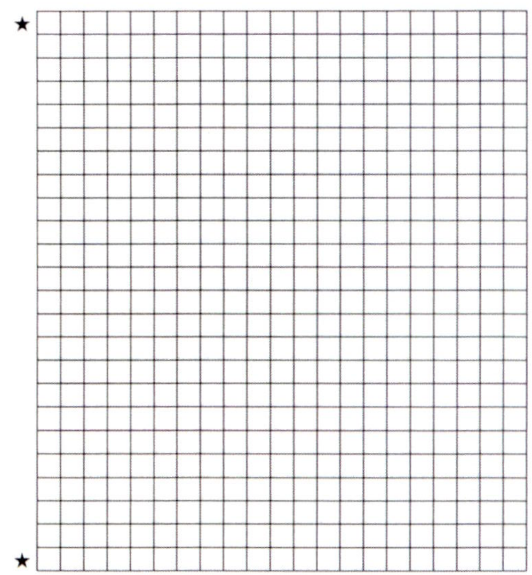

Insert Long Side (89 x 25 threads) (Cut 2)

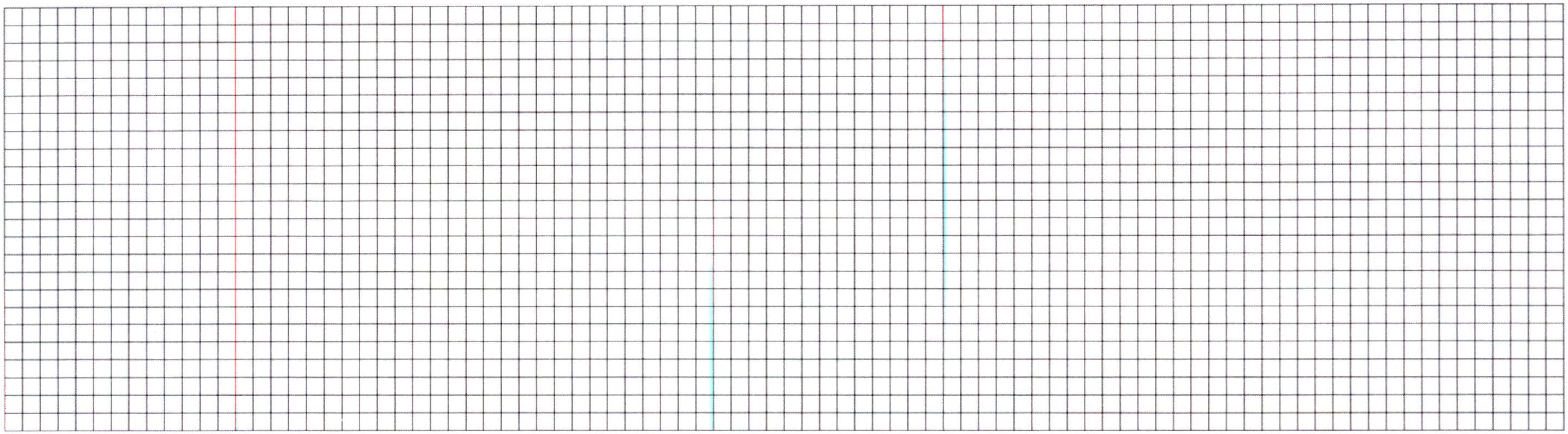

Support (41 x 25 threads)

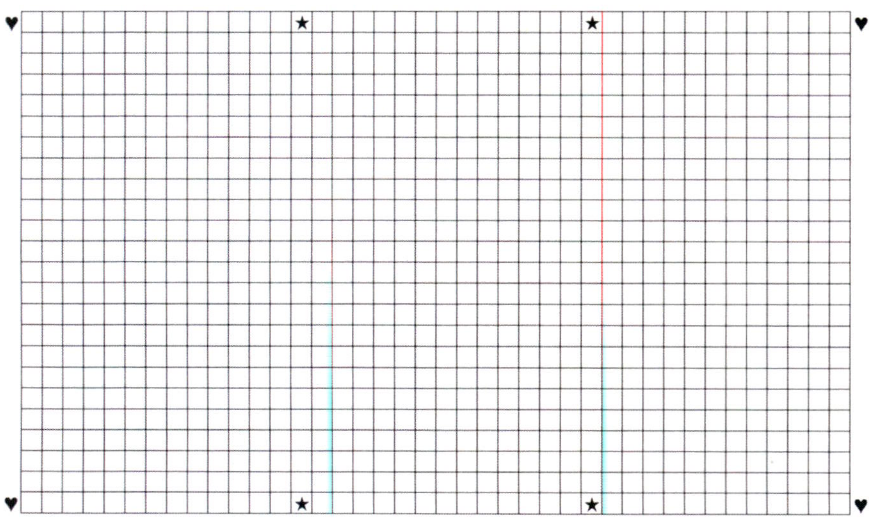

Insert Short Side/Center (45 x 25 threads) (Cut 4)

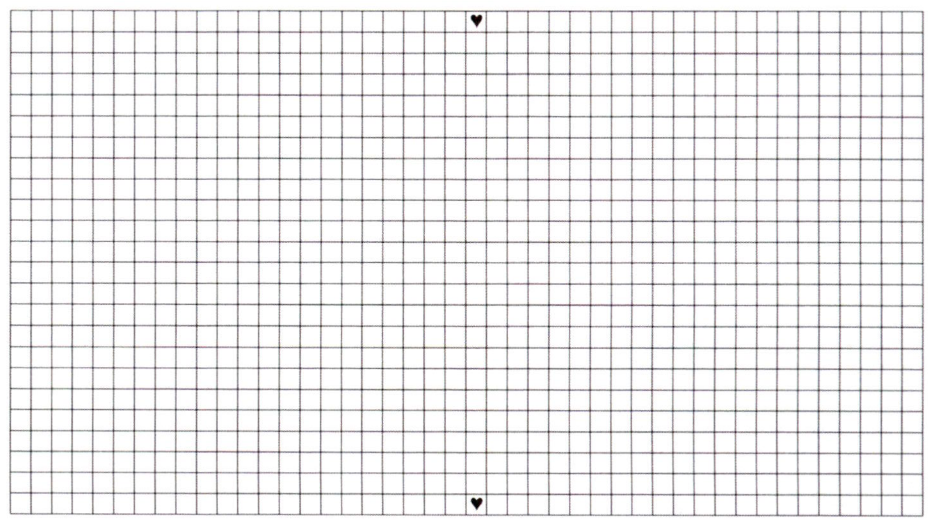

BABY WIPES COVER

NL COLOR

- 20 yellow - 9 yds
- 26 green - 24 yds
- 36 blue - 19 yds
- 41 white - 20 yds
- 41 white Fr. Knot

BABY WIPES COVER

Size: 6"h x $3^1/_2$" dia

Supplies: Worsted weight yarn or Needloft® Plastic Canvas Yarn (refer to color key), one $10^1/_2$" x $13^1/_2$" sheet of clear 7 mesh plastic canvas, and #16 tapestry needle

Stitches Used: French Knot, Gobelin Stitch, Mosaic Stitch, Overcast Stitch, and Tent Stitch

Instructions:

1. Photo model was stitched using worsted weight yarn. Follow chart and use required stitches to work Baby Wipes Cover, leaving stitches in shaded area unworked.
2. Match ▲'s and work stitches in shaded area to join ends of Baby Wipes Cover, forming a cylinder.

Baby Wipes Cover (75 x 39 threads)

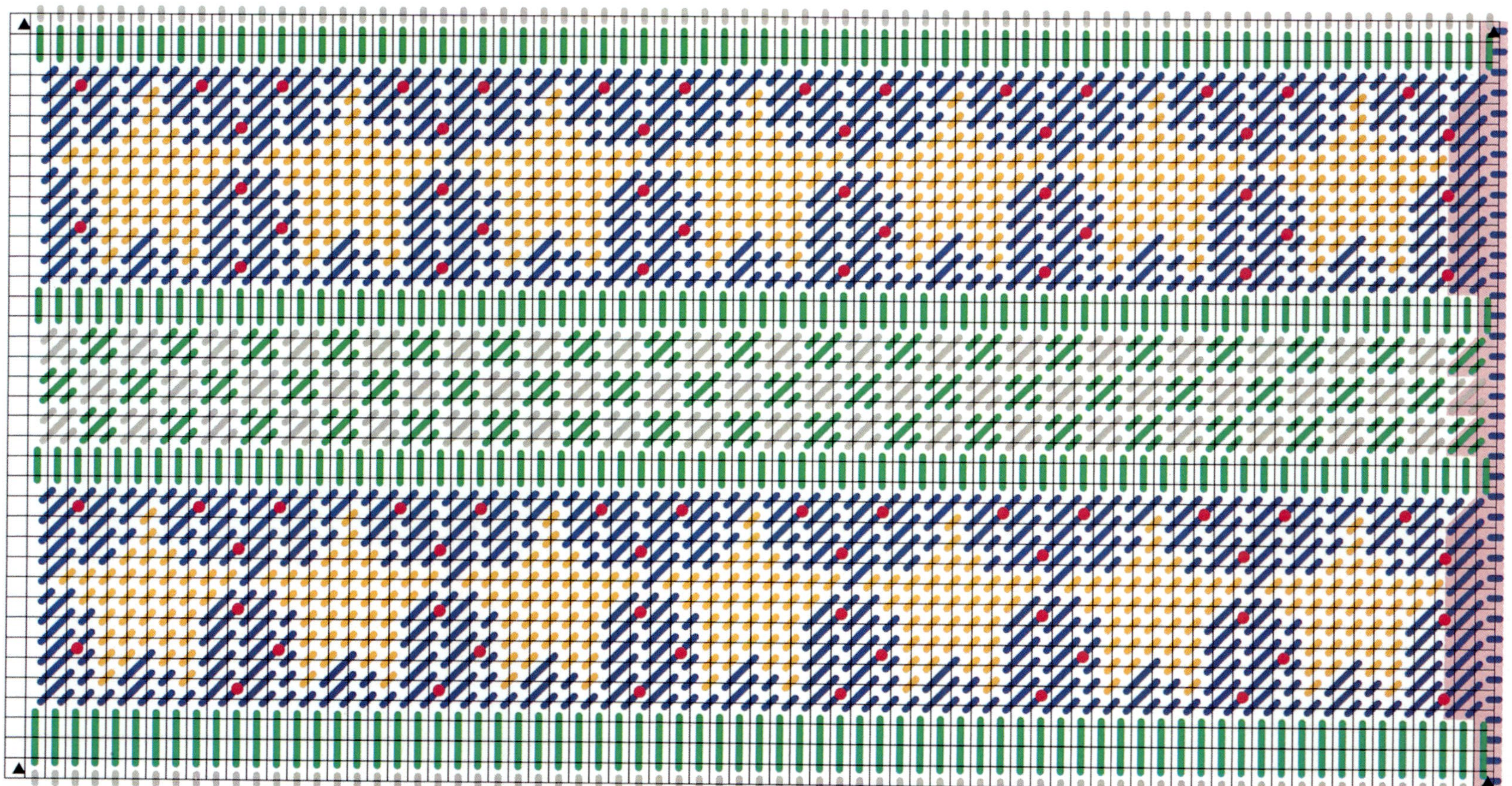

BASKET

NL COLOR

NL	COLOR
17	gold - 2 yds
20	yellow - 25 yds
26	green - 40 yds
36	blue - 44 yds
41	white - 48 yds
56	flesh - 2 yds
*	black Fr. Knot
41	white Fr. Knot
17	gold Fringe

*Use 2-ply yarn.

Diagram

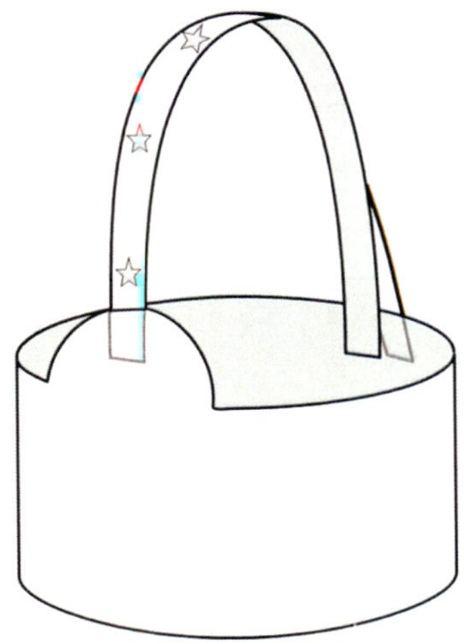

Star (9 x 9 threads) (Stitch 5)

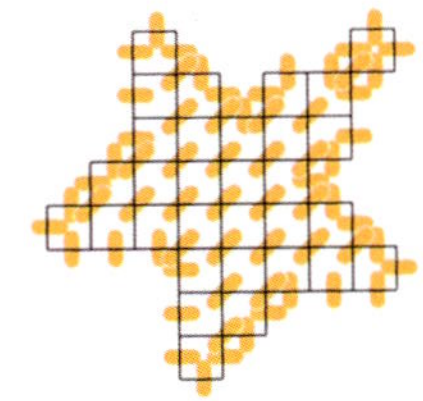

Bottom (44 x 44 threads)

BASKET
Size: 9½"h x 6¾" dia
Supplies: Worsted weight yarn or Needloft® Plastic Canvas Yarn (refer to color keys), three 10½" x 13½" sheets of clear 7 mesh plastic canvas, #16 tapestry needle, and one 1" pink pom-pom
Stitches Used: Backstitch, Diagonal Mosaic Stitch, French Knot, Fringe Stitch, Gobelin Stitch, Mosaic Stitch, Overcast Stitch, Scotch Stitch, and Tent Stitch
Instructions:
1. Photo model was stitched using worsted weight yarn. Follow chart and use required stitches to work Handle through two thicknesses, leaving stitches in shaded area unworked. Follow charts and use required stitches to work remaining Basket pieces, leaving stitches in shaded areas unworked. For bangs on Baby, separate each strand of Fringe into plies. Refer to photo and use needle to separate plies until the desired look is achieved.
2. Match ▲'s and ■'s and work stitches in shaded areas to join Front to Back. Refer to Diagram and match ◆'s to place top side of Handle on right side of Back. Work stitches in shaded area of Handle to join Handle to Back through three thicknesses. Match ★'s to place Handle on wrong side of Front. Work stitches in shaded area to join Handle to Front.
3. Join Bottom to Front and Back using white yarn.
4. Refer to photo for placement and use white yarn to tack side and bottom edge of Cloud to Front. Tack pom-pom to Front using pink yarn. Tack Stars to Handle using yellow yarn. Insert Baby between Cloud and Front.

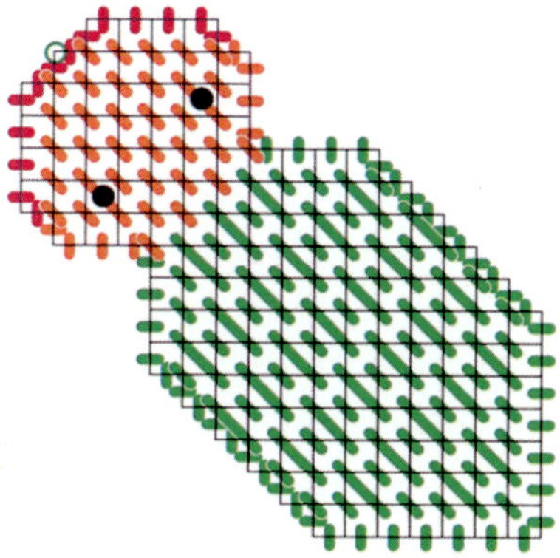

Baby (17 x 17 threads)

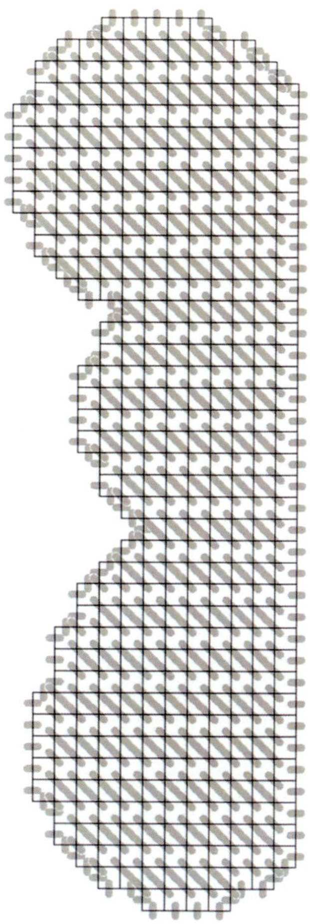

Cloud (42 x 14 threads)

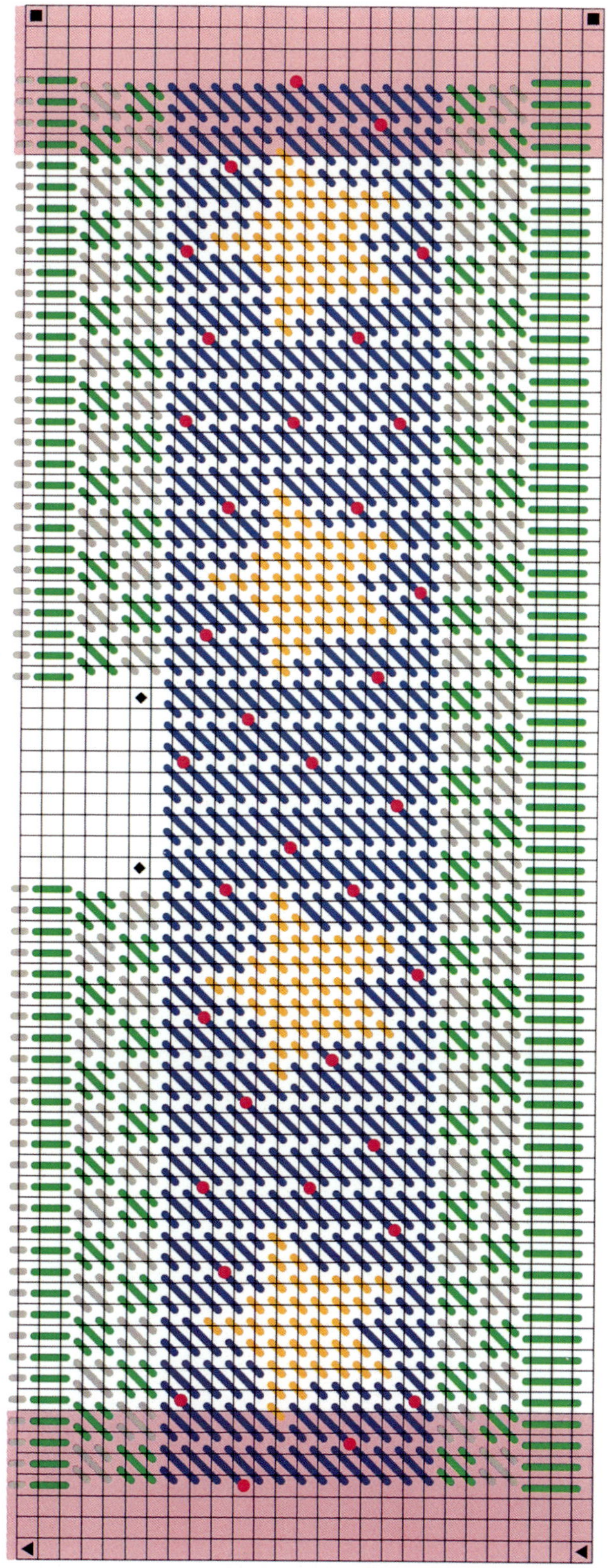

Back (74 x 28 threads)

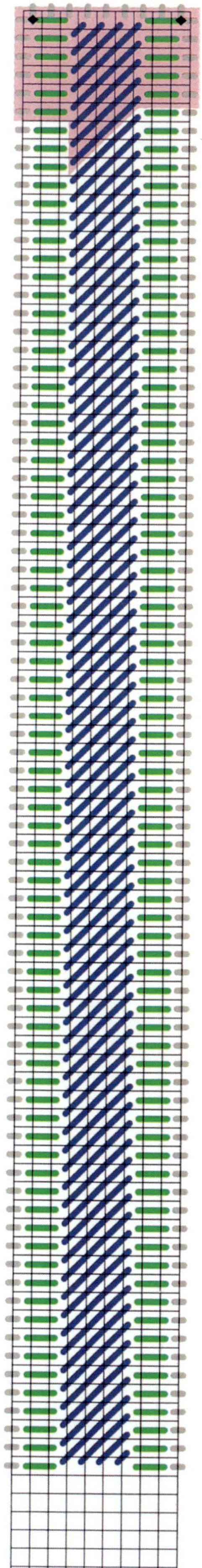

Handle (88 x 10 threads) (Cut 2)

NL	COLOR
00	black - 2 yds
07	pink - 2 yds
20	yellow
26	green
36	blue
41	white
41	white Fr. Knot

Front (76 x 42 threads)

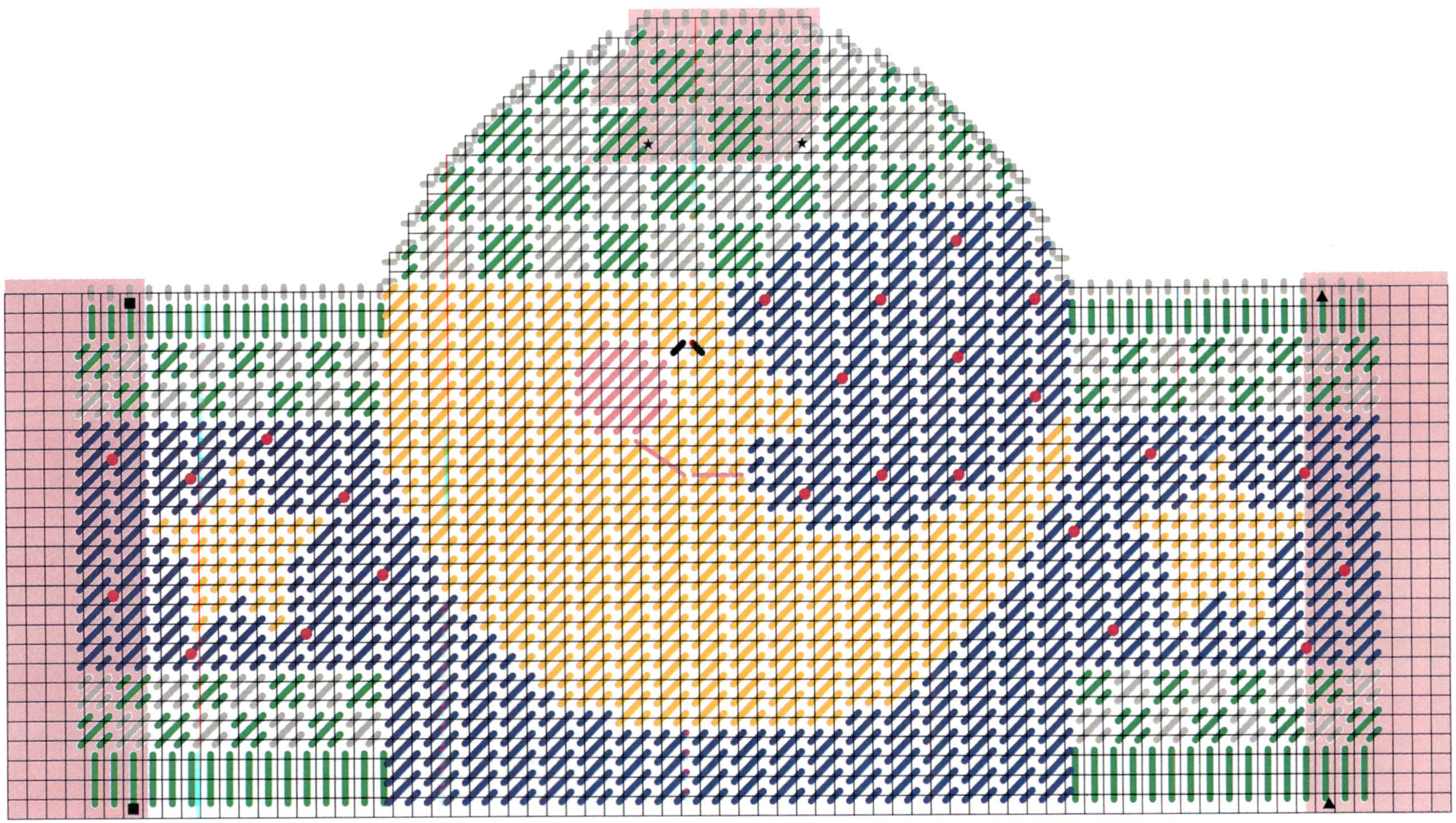

NL COLOR

- 20 yellow - 9 yds
- 26 green - 35 yds
- 36 blue - 15 yds
- 41 white - 9 yds
- 41 white Fr. Knot

Spine (10 x 51 threads)

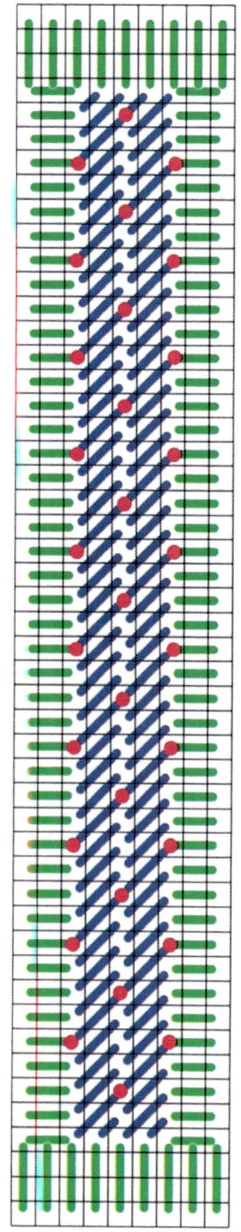

Front/Back (31 x 51 threads) (Stitch 2)

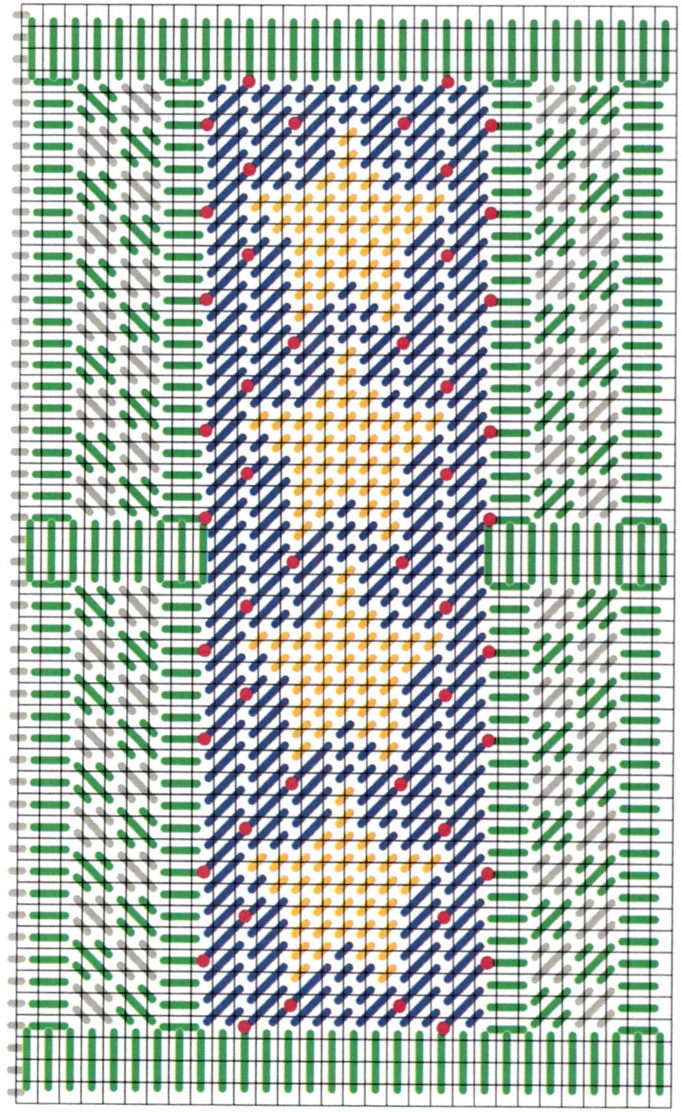

VIDEO CASSETTE TAPE HOLDER

Size: 4¾"w x 7¾"h x 1½"d

*(**Note:** Holds one VHS video cassette tape.)*

Supplies: Worsted weight yarn or Needloft® Plastic Canvas Yarn (refer to color key), one 10½" x 13½" sheet of clear 7 mesh plastic canvas, and #16 tapestry needle

Stitches Used: French Knot, Gobelin Stitch, Mosaic Stitch, Overcast Stitch, and Tent Stitch

Instructions:

1. Photo model was stitched using worsted weight yarn. Follow charts and use required stitches to work Video Cassette Tape Holder pieces.

2. Use white for all joining. Join Spine to Front and Back along long edges of Spine. Join Top and Bottom to Front, Back, and Spine.

3. Cover unworked edges of Top and Bottom with white Overcast Stitches.

Top/Bottom (31 x 10 threads) (Stitch 2)

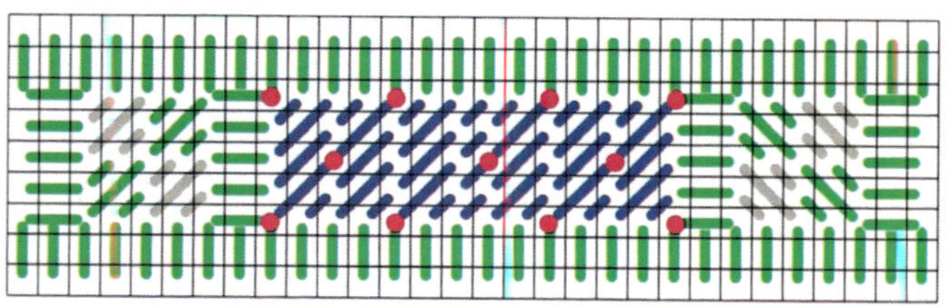

STAR HANGER

NL	COLOR
07	pink - 2 yds
20	yellow - 40 yds
26	green - 11 yds
00	black Fr. Knot - 1 yd

STAR HANGER
Size: 14½"w x 10¾"h
Supplies: Worsted weight yarn or Needloft® Plastic Canvas Yarn (refer to color key), one 10½" x 13½" sheet of clear 7 mesh plastic canvas, #16 tapestry needle, one 1" pink pom-pom, six ½" pink pom-poms, one 14" length of ½" dia wooden dowel, two 25mm dia white wood beads with ½" dia hole, five drapery hooks, one 24" length of ⅜"w pink satin ribbon, two 12" lengths of ⅜"w pink satin ribbon, and clear-drying craft glue
Stitches Used: Backstitch, French Knot, Gobelin Stitch, Overcast Stitch, Scotch Stitch, and Tent Stitch
Instructions:
1. Photo model was stitched using worsted weight yarn. Follow chart and use required stitches to work Star Hanger. Work stitches indicated by double lines on chart by inserting needle in same holes twice for complete coverage.
2. Refer to photo to glue one bead on each end of dowel. Tack dowel to wrong side of Star Hanger using yellow yarn. Insert drapery hooks in Star Hanger at ■'s. Glue pom-poms to Star Hanger and drapery hooks.
3. Refer to photo for placement and glue each end of 24" length of ribbon to back side of dowel. Tie each 12" length of ribbon in a bow around each end of dowel.

Star Hanger (78 x 71 threads)

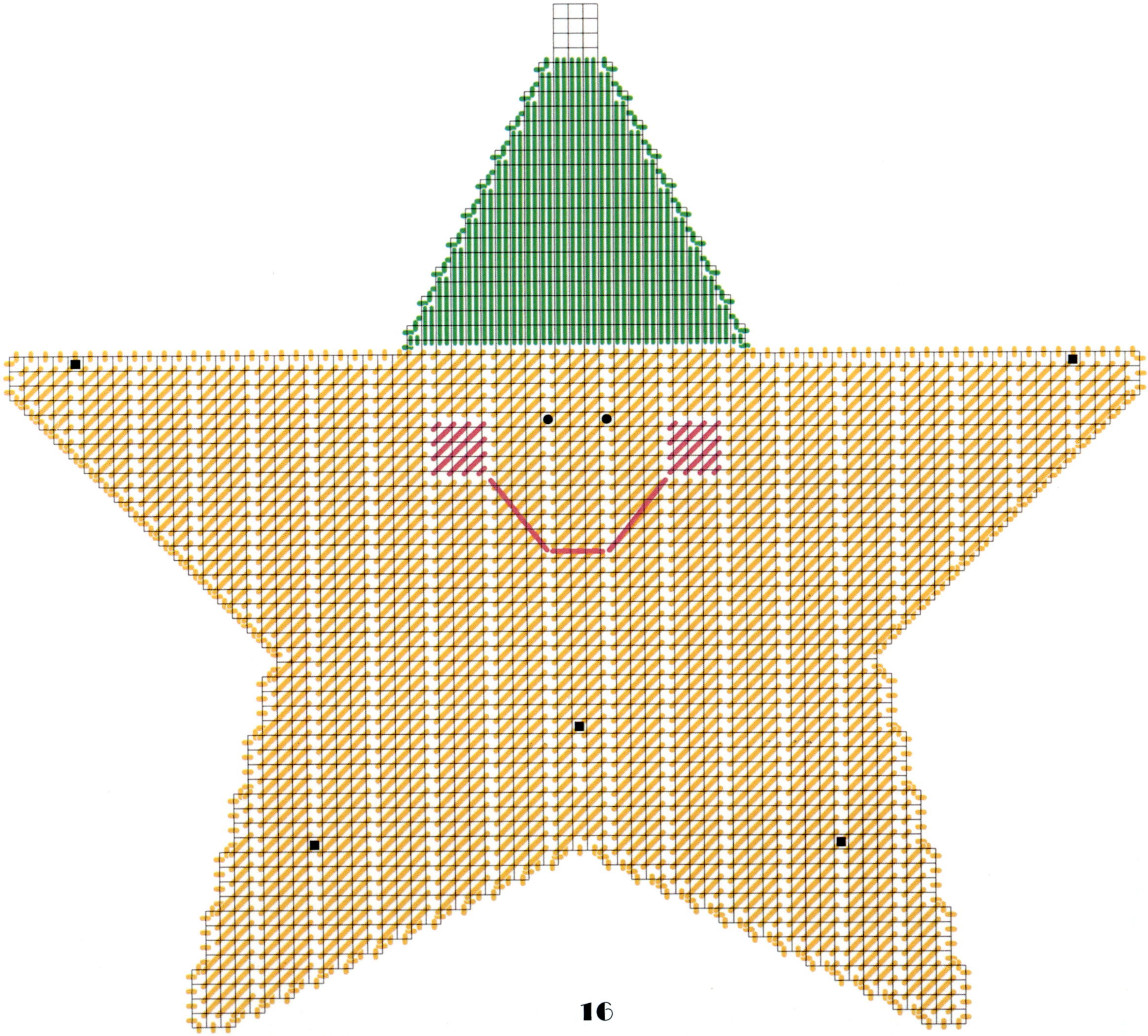

PHOTO FRAME

NL	COLOR	NL	COLOR
07	pink - 1 yd	*	black Fr. Knot - 1 yd
20	yellow - 10 yds	41	white Fr. Knot - 1 yd
26	green - 2 yds		
36	blue - 3 yds		

*Use 2-ply yarn.

Front (36 x 37 threads)

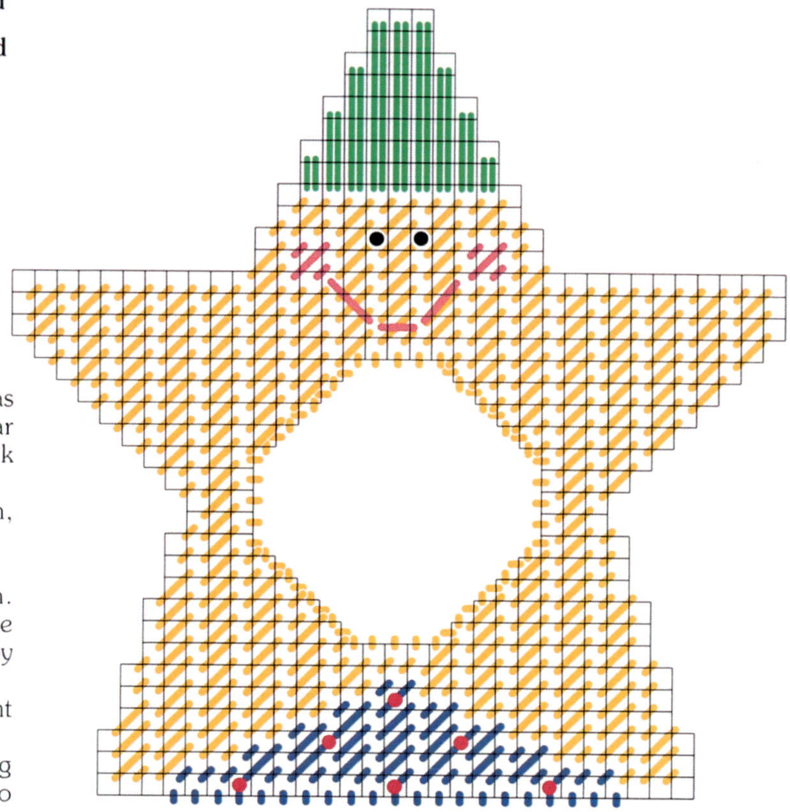

PHOTO FRAME
Size: 5½"w x 5½"h x 3"d
Opening Size: 1⅞"w x 1⅞"h
Supplies: Worsted weight yarn or Needloft® Plastic Canvas Yarn (refer to color key), one 10½" x 13½" sheet of clear 7 mesh plastic canvas, #16 tapestry needle, one ½" pink pom-pom, and one ¼" pink pom-pom
Stitches Used: Backstitch, French Knot, Gobelin Stitch, Mosaic Stitch, Overcast Stitch, and Tent Stitch
Instructions:

1. Photo model was stitched using worsted weight yarn. Follow charts and use required stitches to work Photo Frame pieces. Work stitches indicated by double lines on chart by inserting needle in same holes twice for complete coverage.
2. Refer to photo for placement and tack pom-poms to Front using pink yarn.
3. Join long edges of Stand pieces to Back between ◆'s using yellow yarn. Use yarn color to match closest stitching area to join Front to Back along unworked edges.

Stand (18 x 33 threads) (Cut 2)

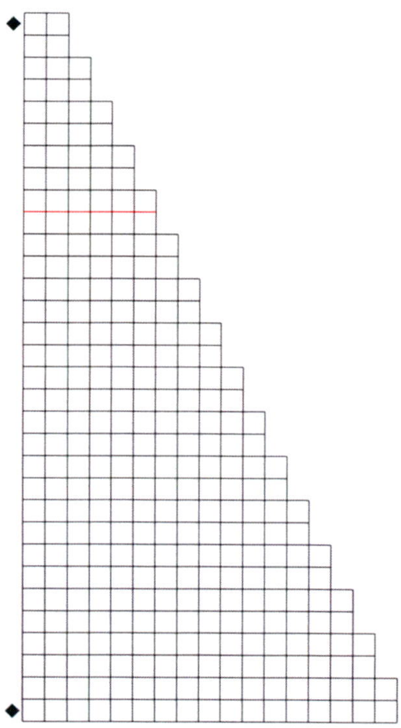

Back (36 x 37 threads)

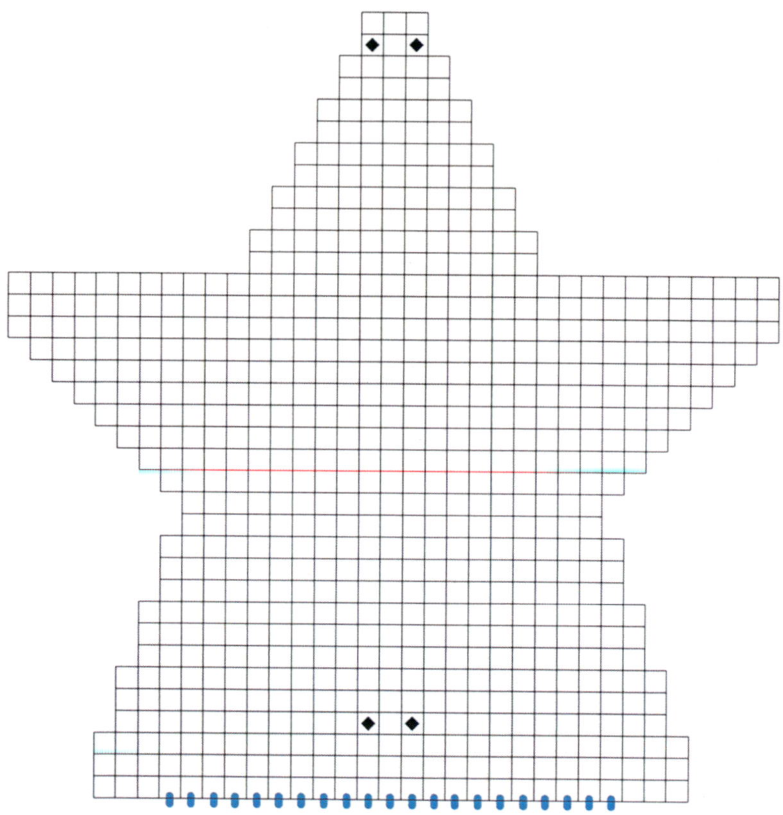

WORKING WITH PLASTIC CANVAS

The projects in this leaflet are worked on 10½" x 13½" sheets of 7 mesh plastic canvas.

Throughout this leaflet, the lines of the canvas will be referred to as threads. However, they are not actually "threads" since the canvas is nonwoven. To cut plastic canvas pieces accurately, count **threads** (not **holes**) as shown in **Fig. 1**.

Fig. 1

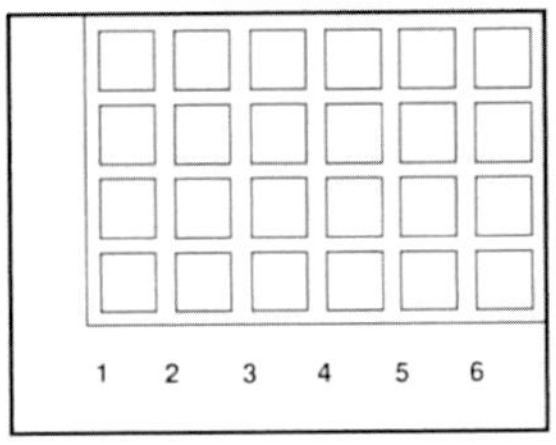

If you find it necessary to mark on the canvas, use a china marker or a grease pencil. Outline shape with marker, cut out shape, and remove markings with a dry tissue.

For some pieces, it is important to keep both sides of your work looking neat. Using longer strands will help avoid excessive yarn ends. Be careful to completely hide yarn ends under previously worked stitches.

Plastic canvas is washable, but acrylic yarn must be used if washing is desired. Plastic canvas cannot be professionally dry–cleaned or put in a clothes dryer.

Use a #26 tapestry needle when working with nylon line. To prevent nylon line from slipping out of needle, tie end of line in a knot at eye of needle. Secure nylon line at beginning and end of stitching by tying several knots on back of piece.

WORKING WITH YARN

To help you select colors for your projects, we have included numbers for Needloft® Plastic Canvas Yarn in our color key. The headings in the color keys are for Needloft® Yarn (**NL**) and the descriptive color name (**COLOR**). Needloft® Yarn is suitable only for 7 mesh plastic canvas.

Worsted weight yarn is used for the projects in this leaflet. Worsted weight yarn has four plies which are twisted together to form one strand. When the instructions indicate 2-ply yarn, separate the strand of yarn and stitch using only two of the four plies.

Needloft® Yarn will not easily separate. When the instructions call for "2-ply", we recommend that you substitute with six strands of embroidery floss.

It is important to buy all of the yarn you need to complete your project at the same time. Yarn often varies in the amount of dye used to color the yarn. Although the variation may be slight when yarns from two different dye lots are held together, the variation is usually very apparent on a stitched piece.

STITCH DIAGRAMS

Bring threaded needle up at 1 and all odd numbers and down at 2 and all even numbers.

BACKSTITCH

This stitch is worked over completed stitches to outline or define ***(Fig. 2)***. It is sometimes worked over more than one thread. Backstitch may also be used to cover canvas.

Fig. 2

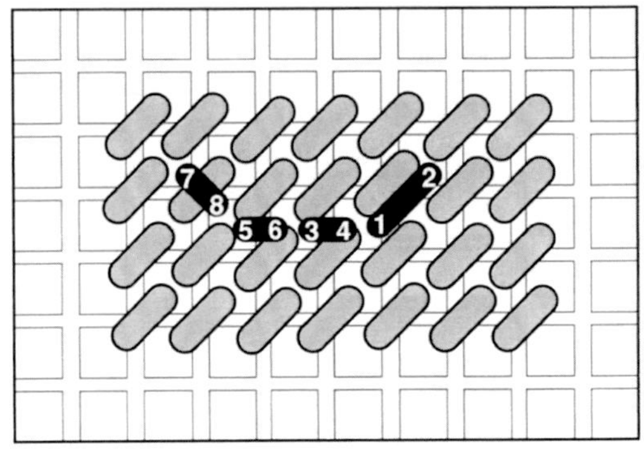

DIAGONAL MOSAIC STITCH

A variation of the Mosaic Stitch, this stitch is worked in diagonal rows as shown in **Fig. 3**.

Fig. 3

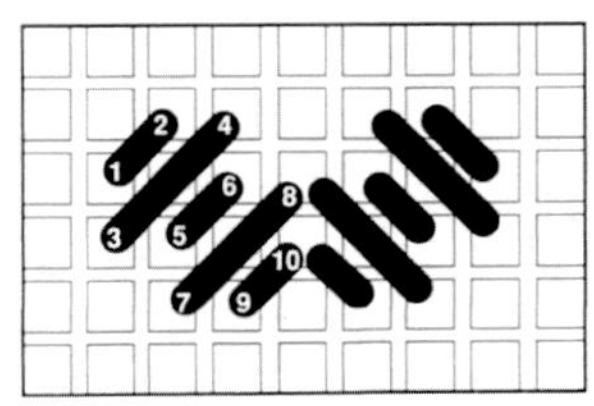

FRENCH KNOT

Bring needle up through hole. Wrap yarn once around needle and insert needle in same hole, holding end of yarn with non-stitching fingers ***(Fig. 4)***. Tighten knot; then pull needle through canvas, holding yarn until it must be released.

Fig. 4

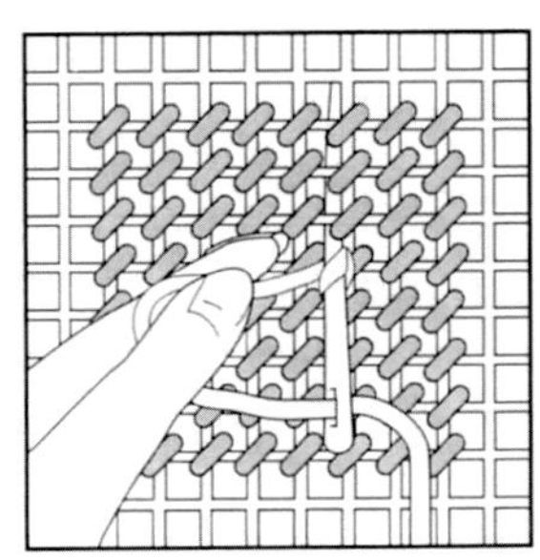

FRINGE STITCH

Fold an 8" length of yarn in half. Thread needle with loose ends of yarn. Take needle down at 1, leaving a 1" loop on top of the canvas. Come up at 2, bring needle through loop, and pull tightly ***(Fig. 5)***. Trim strands 1/2" from knot. A dot of glue on back of fringe will help keep stitches in place.

Fig. 5

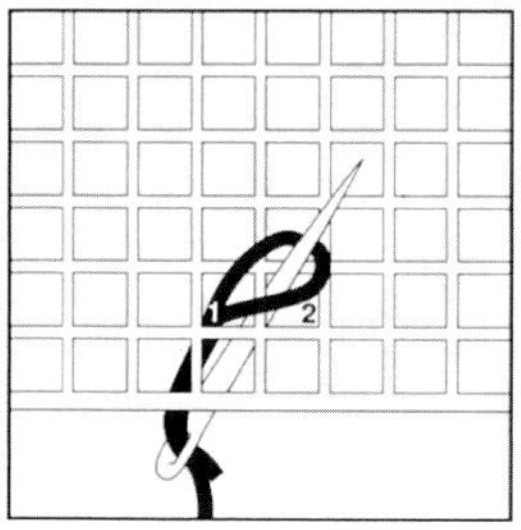

GOBELIN STITCH

This basic straight stitch is worked over two or more threads or intersections. The number of threads or intersections may vary according to the chart ***(Fig. 6)***.

Fig. 6

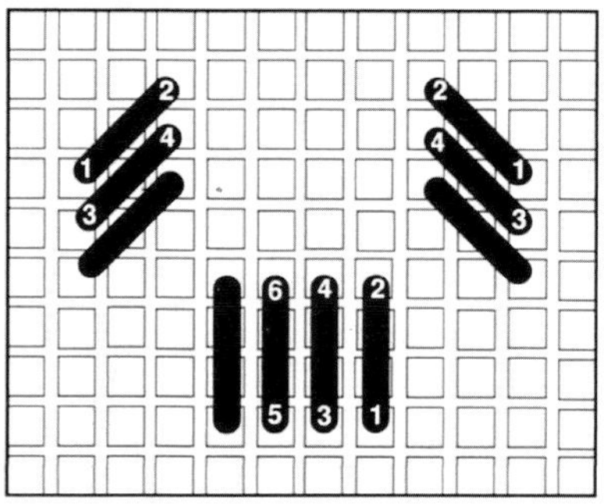

MOSAIC STITCH

This three stitch pattern forms small squares ***(Fig. 7)***.

Fig. 7

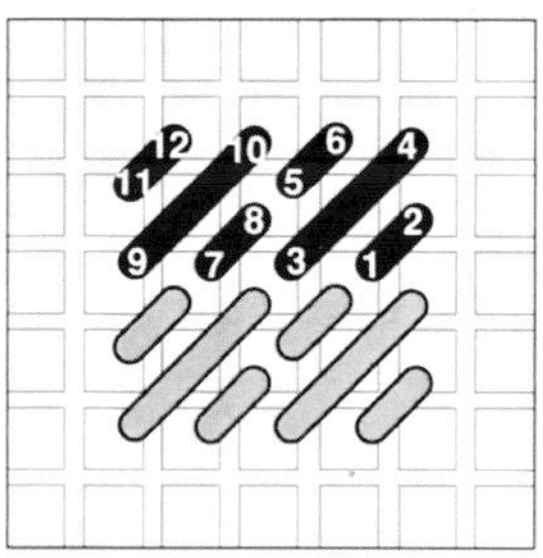

OVERCAST STITCH

This stitch covers the edge of the canvas and joins pieces of canvas ***(Fig. 8)***. It may be necessary to go through the same hole more than once to get an even coverage on the edge, especially at the corners.

Fig. 8

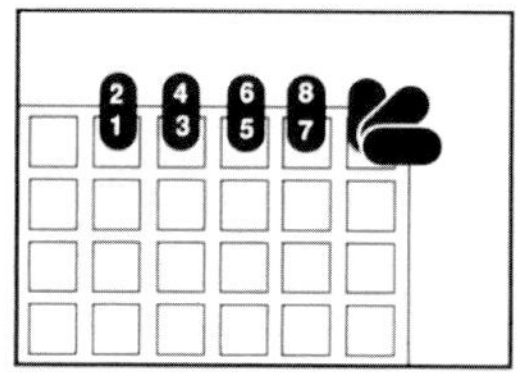

SCOTCH STITCH

This stitch may be worked over three or more threads and forms a square. **Fig. 9** shows it worked over four threads.

Fig. 9

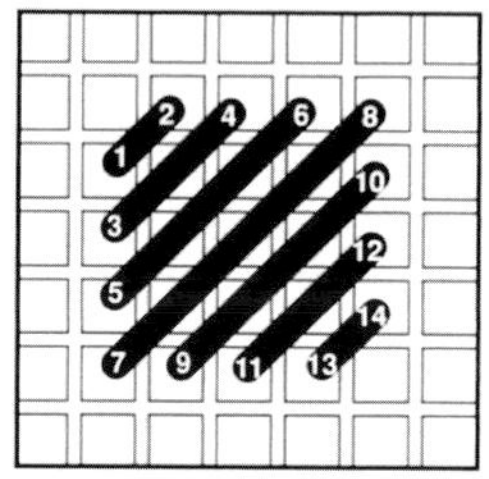

TENT STITCH

This stitch is worked over one intersection as shown in **Fig. 10.** Refer to **Fig. 11** to work the **Reversed Tent Stitch**.

Fig. 10

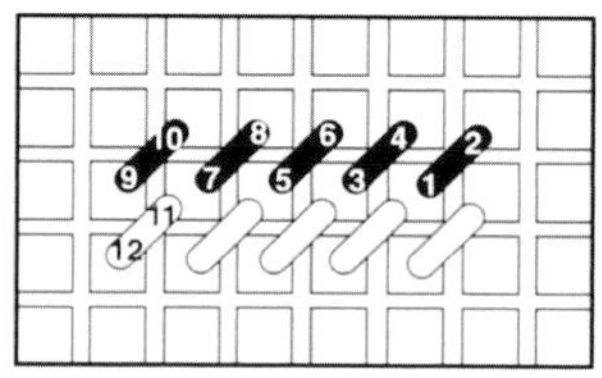

Fig. 11

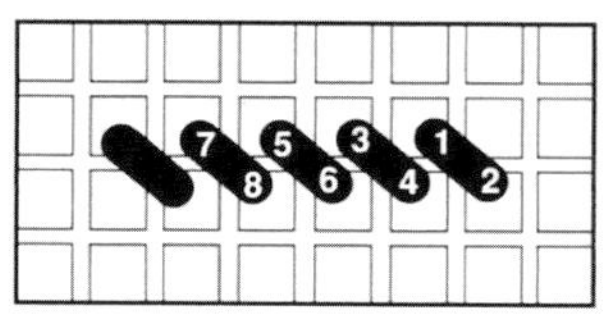

A STAR IS BORN

GENERAL INSTRUCTIONS

1. Fig. 1, page 18, shows how to count threads accurately. Follow charts to cut out pieces.

2. Backstitches used for detail ***(Fig. 2**, page 18**)*** and French Knots ***(Fig. 4**, page 18**)*** are worked over completed stitches.

3. Overcast Stitches ***(Fig. 8)*** are used to cover edges of pieces and to join pieces.

Instructions tested and cover items made by Virginia Cates and Janice Gordon.

Show us what you're working on!

Share your project photos with us on social media.
Tag us @leisureartsinc or use #leisurearts

Made in U.S.A.